A World Turned Upside Down

A Chronicle of Life and Times in 2020

Poems by

W.G. Perry

A World Turned Upside Down

Copyright © 2020 W.G. Perry

Library of Congress Control Number: 2020918677

ISBN: 9798675126798

A World Turned Upside Down

For those who suffered from the COVID-19 pandemic

and

In memory of those who died at its behest

A World Turned Upside Down

A World Turned Upside Down

CONTENTS

Introduction

A WORLD TURNED UPSIDE DOWN

On January 1, 2020 we rang in the new year.
Acknowledging the world's challenges, we focused on good cheer.
Most families had celebrated a prior year-end holiday.
As work and school resumed, we returned to our routines in a
    habitual way.

Looking out to the future, high school seniors embarked on ski
    trips before planning their proms.
College seniors began honing in on graduation alongside proud
    dads and moms.
With unemployment rates down and the stock market high,
Individuals planned family vacations, as well as new cars or homes
    to buy.

On Valentine's Day few suspected a novel coronavirus lurking.
News dribbling in from China about pneumonia-like symptoms
    sounded quirky.
Few knew a virus in Wuhan was surreptitiously working.
We had heard of SARS and MERS, but what we knew was murky.

Stories of a deadly virus passing from animals to humans in a
    Wuhan market began to abound.
U.S. travel to China was halted, so experts were asked to expound.
Before long COVID-19 swirled through the world without a sound.
We woke up in March to find a world turned upside down.

THE PANDEMIC

April 2, 2020

Unpredictable events in extraordinary times halt activities
    cluttering up our lives.
We work from home, distance ourselves, and reduce gears from
    high drive.
Uncanny speed of events enables denial as anxieties ensue.
We learn "flattening the curve" concepts our governments pursue.

When we peer out our windows, we see sunshine on high,
But inside walls of each abode, we listen to news reports and sigh.
When COVID-19 case counts climb, we feel creeping unease.
We hear partisan perspectives color the ubiquity of this disease.

Sheltered at home we step back, giving ourselves reprieve,
To reflect on where we are as a nation, who we are as a people,
    and in what we believe.
What happens to the homeless while the rest of us stay at home?
To whom should they address pandemic concerns as they roam?

Are we practicing survival of the fittest as we stockpile our
    shelves?
Or, are we thinking about our neighbors instead of just ourselves?
Are we pondering who will be awarded that last ICU hospital bed?
Or, are we finding ways to support our health care workers and
    keep the needy fed?

It gives us pause to be unable to predict how severe the pandemic
    will be.
And, it's unsettling to deal with increasing uncertainty.
The pandemic reminds us of science fiction movies or a terrifying
    tale.
As we tackle challenges before us, let's hope our better angels
    prevail.

RED OR BLUE

April 8, 2020

Aspects of our beliefs seemed certain, like the afterglow of
    twilight.
While we slept transformation seeped upon our world making us
    contrite.
Did our convictions mutate, deviating to indict?
We ponder whether our brothers and sisters will ever reunite.

Do we love our country, the most resourceful on God's earth?
Do we take pride in our Constitution, willed by founding fathers
    since our nation's birth?
Do we revere the brave who venture into harm's way?
Do we protect our children on any given day?
Do we value the air we breathe during our tenure on this land?
Do we reach out to our neighbors to lend a helping hand?

When did seeming certainties become subjectively contentious?
    Who knew?
Why do so many discourses diverge to variations of red or blue?

VOTE

April 11, 2020

On February third in the year 1870, Amendment XV was dated.
This Constitutional amendment stated,
The right of citizens to vote could not be denied
"…on account of race, color, or previous conditions of servitude…"
     it decried.

On August 18th in the year 1920, Amendment XIX was slated.
Its long-awaited ratification indicated,
The right of citizens to vote could not be denied
"…on account of sex…" our Constitution belatedly applied.

We read the words in these documents or copies thereof.
We hear the law repeated from courts high above.
Yet 150 years pass and the right to vote is still debated.
We ponder motivation for voting rules ostensibly re-created.

"Excuse me sir, I see no validity to your photo ID."
"Excuse me 'mam, your polling place is across town next to a
     weeping willow tree."
"Excuse me boy, the line is long so you best get back to work."
"Excuse me girl, college addresses don't count, it is a voting
     quirk."
"Excuse me citizens, polls are closed as coronaviruses lurk."

Don't we want to do everything we can to promote voting as a way
     to strengthen our democracy?
The founding fathers abhorred a monarchy and feared an
     aristocracy.
Voting represents a long fought right.
In a country like ours it is democracy's shining light.

EASTER

April 12, 2020

We'll miss services at church,
COVID-19 keeps us away.
Treatments and vaccines await research,
At home without family or friends we stay.
And so, we pray.

The sick in need of dire care
Hope to make it through another day.
Nurses and doctors without PPE to spare,
We can never fully repay.
And so, we pray.

The virus doesn't discriminate by ethnicities or age.
On young, old, black, white, it may prey.
"Social distancing" said the public health sage,
Must hold the virus at bay.
And so, we pray.

In the resurrection many believe,
While spring buds a rebirth of a delicate bouquet.
Faith gives us reprieve,
May God make house calls today.
And so, we pray.

WHAT ROCKS OUR NATION

April 17, 2020

Past tragedies and calamities have rocked our nation.
We bear witness to earthquakes, tornadoes, floods, and many a
    conflagration.
The wrath of hurricanes like Sandy, Katrina, and Irma we knew,
As well as H1N1, SARS, MERS, Ebola, and Spanish Flu.

Just when we thought we had experienced every shocking scare,
Covid-19 emerged from our dreams like an alarming nightmare.
We count the additional cases and deaths each day,
Praying for vaccines without delay.

Officials of all stripes bicker about state and federal powers,
To open the economy before a bull market sours.
22 million people are unemployed to date.
After the SBA ran out of money small businesses fear their fate.

We are the country that put a man on the moon,
The wealthiest nation where many made a fortune.
With some of the finest research universities in the world,
We long for the mystery of this virus to be unfurled.

May this insidious disease stop its attacking,
Deleterious chaos in our homeland is wracking.
Experts advise we test, test, test and pursue contact tracing,
Until what now rocks our nation halts its racing.

AN ENIGMA

April 20, 2020

An enigmatic man's birthday would have been today,
It has been years since he passed away.
He had a passion for world history, yes, he did,
Countless times he cited historical events when I was just a kid.

He told stories about three cultures living peacefully in Spain,
The rise and fall of European kings and each dramatic reign.
He lived through the challenging terms of twelve U.S. presidents.
In his twilight years he could opine about these White House
    residents.

What would this sage think about our dual crises worldwide?
The COVID-19 pandemic and the economic slide.
Stay at home or open businesses—two forces about to collide.
He'd tell us to study the pillars of history and then decide.

EARTH DAY

April 22, 2020

Earth Days focused on recycling and composting in eras before
    Twitter,
Bottle deposits and enforcement of fines for scattering litter.
Speakers enlightened us about solar, wind, and reduction of a
    carbon footprint,
As climate change experts initiated their imprint.

On this Earth Day 2020 there will be no parades,
No outward celebrations, only virtual charades.
As the Paris Climate Agreement sojourned, now a topic of the past,
We could not have anticipated today's newsworthy items could
    make us feel aghast.

Covid-19 struck 800,000+ in the U.S. and 42,000+ have died.
U.S. data appears higher than that of any other nation, so
    experts decried.
People from inside and outside the U.S. look on with disbelief.
Why can't our health care workers get sufficient supplies and a
    little relief?

A global pandemic brought our prospering economy to a halt.
Despite federal intervention, 26 million U.S. jobless claims
    may cause many to default.
Direction from state and federal governments can be incongruous,
    to say the least.
Some state bans on opening hair salons, massage parlors, and
    tattoo shops have been released.

States promoting testing and shelter-within take the heat,
Fractious factions form, their mantras replete.
China donates an additional $30,000,000 to the World Health
    Organization,
While America's timing of its plan to suspend WHO funds is
    viewed by many as an abomination.

The U.S. played a unique role for decades after World War II,
Setting a profound example of all the good a democracy could do.
Its power, prosperity, and values made the U.S. exceptional—
    ideals others wanted to emulate.
Can its position in the world be restored before it's too late?

On this Earth Day 2020 we don't know our fate,
We expect few Earth Day protests, marches, or much debate.
The pandemic shines a spotlight on issues that loom,
Well-prepared hospital systems, leadership, reliance on science—
    none of which we can presume.

75th ANNIVERSARY OF LIBERATION DAY IN ITALY

April 25, 2020

April 25 marks the 75th anniversary of Italy's Liberation by Allied
    forces after World War II,
Waving Italian flags, citizens of Rome sang an Italian resistance
    song they well knew.
Under lockdown to curb the spread of COVID-19,
Citizens singing from windows and balconies--a touching scene.

For 60 million Italians, April 25th retains an unforgettable scar,
Benito Mussolini aligned himself with Hitler as a fascist avatar.
"Il Duce" hanging upside down at Milan's Piazzale Loreto, not a
    pleasant image today,
So many Italians experienced brutalities during that era, the
    suffering remains at bay.

On April 25, 2020 jet planes flew in formations across Rome's
    blue skies.
Other festivities were cancelled amidst the uncertainty, fear, and
    somber cries.
In 2020 Italy has been fighting a war of a different kind,
A battle unanticipated and unclearly defined.

Italy's mysterious enemy amassed nearly 200,000 cases,
Throughout northern Italy before seeking the country's southern
    faces.
The COVID-19 adversary struck so hard Italians questioned
    whether they'd survive.
By Liberation Day 2020, COVID-19 claimed 26,000+ Italian lives.

Sheltered within, Italians took to their windows and doors,
Singing "Bella Ciao," a resistance song against invaders and wars.
We pray for our Italian friends who we'll never forget,
And, hope the magic of Italy will return or at least be reset.

MAY DAY

May 1, 2020

May Day means different things to different folks,
For millennia celebrating the change in seasons is what May 1
    evokes.
Medieval times featured dances with ribbons and streamers around
    a May pole,
Years later treat-filled baskets on front doors and May queens
    waving to those who'd cajole.

At the peak of the Industrial Revolution in the USA,
Workers united to proclaim on May 1, an eight-hour work day.
Unfortunately, May 1, 1886 was followed by a strike and mayhem
    at the Haymarket Riot,
After the 1894 Pullman Strike, President Grover Cleveland
    decided U.S. tremors needed to quiet.

The U.S. celebration of Labor Day was officially moved to the first
    Monday in September,
Severing ties with international workers' rallies so that citizens
    would cease to remember.
In 1958 Dwight D. Eisenhower sought for May 1 to undergo a
    novel reinvention,
He declared May 1 "Law Day," honoring the place of law in our
    country's ascension.

There is another "mayday" term we may foresee.
This "mayday" is derived from a French phrase "M'aidez!"
    meaning "Help me."
Stated three times this "mayday" conveys a life-threatening signal
    of distress,
A crucial imperative, listeners must expeditiously address.

How will history judge May Day 2020?
A tragic worldwide pandemic with rising fear a plenty,
The U.S. has 1,082,000+ cases and 63,000+ dead,
On six of seven continents nearly 3,303,000+ cases and
    235,000+ deaths, bring us additional dread.

"Businesses must open!"— "Businesses stay closed!"
More testing is needed yet the whereabouts of reagents is not
    easily exposed.
Supply chains for medical composites often reside in other lands,
Not readily available to laboratories' hands.

Many sheltered within and social distanced for six weeks,
Washing hands so many times, their cleanliness squeaks.
Masks, latex gloves, disinfectant wipes—some experts
    recommend, others dissuade,
Hoaxes, fake news, disputes, astonishing claims, cacophony never
    seem to fade.

But we have faith and are hopeful that the status quo will pass,
Or a vaccine will be on the horizon at last.
Various doctors say we could be talking about this pandemic a
    year from now.
If so, instead of May Day, it may be "mayday-mayday-mayday"
    we avow.

CINCO DE MAYO

May 5, 2020

This holiday commemorates May 5, 1862, in Mexican history,
During the Franco-Mexican War the Mexican army, against all
    odds, won a battlefield victory.
In the overall war against the French, not a major win,
The event bolstered the country's resistance, causing the
    opposition chagrin.

Now a relatively minor holiday in Mexico, Cinco de Mayo, or the
    Battle of Puebla Day,
Evolved into a celebration of Mexican culture and heritage around
    the world, including the USA.
How will this holiday be celebrated on May 5, 2020?
Across cities and countries, COVID-19 strikes young and old alike
    harming so many.

Will we see pinatas, maracas, Mexican hat dances, or folks
    drinking margaritas?
How many will eat burritos, chalupas, sopes, flan, or fajitas?
While 37 million Mexican-American residents comprise 11+% of
    the U.S. population,
Current events may disrupt the typical Cinco de Mayo celebration.

Mexico's COVID-19 strategy is to contain and deport,
A population of nearly 129 million has had nearly 25,000 cases
    and 2200+ deaths to report.
The contagion curves in the U.S. and Mexico are weeks apart,
Collaboration between neighbors could save lives and give medical
    suppliers a head start.

U.S. officials urge Mexico to open its economy so North America
    can attain
Little disruption to U.S. manufacturing supply chains.
How many U.S. companies' manufacturing orders
Depend on component parts produced south of the border?

What if Mexico doesn't follow the country's COVID-19 curve and
    its own quarantine?
U.S. companies in Mexico may report more strikes, deaths,
    disrupted production routines.
During the past several years, the U.S. and Mexico have had a
    tumultuous association,
U.S. and Mexican citizens and Mexican immigrants struggle with
    immigration in each nation.

Activity at U.S. immigration facilities has come to a halt,
Multitudes may be stranded at border town refugee camps awaiting
    COVID-19's assault.
On Cinco de Mayo let's hope both countries work together so
    fewer will suffer,
In this era of the pandemic, lives need a buffer.

STOP...TAKE A BREATH

May 7, 2020

Stop…Take a breath. Close your eyes.
Within the next hour how many people will die?
Stop…Take a breath. Close your eyes.
Will loved ones have time to say their good-byes?

Stop…Take a breath.   Close your eyes.
How do the doctors and nurses hold back their cries?
Stop…Take a breath. Close your eyes.
How do we circumvent a novel coronavirus reprise?

When was the last time we expressed gratitude?
To see
     Vibrant blue skies,
     A stunning sunrise,
     Fluttering butterflies.

When was the last time we granted ourselves solitude?
To hear
     Sweet birds singing,
     Church bells ringing,
     Children at play swinging.

When was the last time we created an interlude?
To feel
     A soft breeze,
     A swaying of trees,
     A water droplet freeze.

When was the last time we gave ourselves latitude?
To smell
     Dew after spring showers,
     Fragrance of garden flowers,
     Grass just mowed for hours.

Stop…Take a breath. Close your eyes.
Let's hold on tight to the people whose love we abide.
Stop…Take a breath. Close your eyes.

MOTHER'S DAY

May 10, 2020

Mother's Day traces back to ancient Roman and Greek festivals
    celebrating mothering day,
In 1914 President Wilson established its significance on the second
    Sunday in May.
On this day in 1968 a march to support the underprivileged was
    hosted by Coretta Scott King,
During the 1970s women's groups used this day to let calls for
    equal rights and childcare ring.

In the year 2020 on this Mother's Day,
What news do we have to relay?
To our mothers living nationwide
Or to our mothers who in heaven reside.

Shall we look for something good like a silver lining?
Among negative events positives can be intertwining.
For example, our crime rates declined and gasoline prices were
    slashed.
U.S. auto accidents decreased and insurance companies refunded
    premiums unabashed.

Due to less pollution many large cities now have clean air.
On expressways no horns blare, no road rage there.
Flights can easily be booked without delay,
We can tele-visit with our doctors on any given day.

Yet, there may be no spring baseball or major sports this year.
No concerts, no theater, no large gatherings due to COVID-19 fear.
Schools and colleges remain online,
Not many church services to visit with the divine.

No tours, nor trips to far off places,
No seeing the children's and grandchildren's smiling faces.
No hair appointments unless we cross a state line,
No family dinners where parents' and children's stories entwine.

On this Mother's Day we see much changed on our earth,
We reminisce about nostalgic eras after our mothers gave birth.
Arch enemy number one, COVID-19, has enveloped us uninvited,
We pray today for a time when mothers and loved ones will be
    reunited.

HOW DID NEW ZEALAND GET IT RIGHT?

May 15, 2020

In this COVID-19 war many countries have struggled each day
    from morning until night,
How did New Zealand manage to get it right?
With less than 5 million people, a country so small,
So far has contained the COVID-19 virus without a cabal.

On March 15, with a mere six cases, the country enacted a
    mandatory quarantine,
For all visitors, it was required and became routine.
Less than two weeks later New Zealand acted decisively, enforcing
    a country-wide lockdown.
Only the most essential workers could be seen in any given town.

By the end of April and into May, New Zealand's case counts were
    looking good,
On May 15, less than 1500 total cases, only one new case, and 21
    deaths indicate where the country stood.
Tourism, the country's largest export industry, suffered more than
    anyone thought it ever could,
If more populated countries were able to so act, how many deaths
    could be spared in our brotherhood?

A FRIEND

May 16, 2020

During the 2020 pandemic as each month merges into the next,
We communicate through email, social media, and texts.
While we make occasional phone calls and listen to news filled
       with doom,
We also treat ourselves to FaceTime or a conversation on Zoom.

There is plenty of time to cook, to do laundry, and other chores.
Once a week we might even venture to grocery stores.
Sheltered within, we have a lot of time to think,
Sometimes our thoughts expand and sometimes they shrink.

It is at these times when our thoughts digress,
We may focus on what we value more, and what we value less.
Do we reflect on objects, events, or places that really don't matter?
If they disappeared would we hear a moment of clatter?

As our thoughts drift, veer, and roam,
They converge to a place closer to our heart and its home.
Maybe we remember someone with whom we shared a
       background or a history in school,
Or a person who knew us when we were considered "cool."

We think about that someone whose smile brings us good cheer,
An individual we entrust with secrets we hold dear.
How about that person with whom we always like to talk?
Or the one who comforts us during a walk.

That selfless mortal who always hears us out,
The one with whom we share our thoughts, explain, vent, or even
       shout,
A caring individual who shows interest in us and what we are all
       about,
Is there such a person who likes us or loves us without any doubt?

While we march on through this pandemic which seems to have no
    end,
Let's put aside all with which we have to contend,
And consider how fortunate we are to have
    Someone upon whom we can depend,
    Someone who will never offend,
    Someone who does not condescend,
    Someone we will always defend,
    Someone who helps us transcend.
Let's never forget how blessed we are to have a friend.

VICTORIA DAY

May 18, 2020

Victoria Day in Canada is a holiday observed on the Monday
    before May 25th each year,
Marking the birthday of Queen Victoria, ruler of the UK and the
    British Empire she did steer.
Queen Victoria reigned for 63 years and almost one more.
In some parts of Canada, the holiday is called "May Two-Four."

"May Two-Four" refers to the date the holiday falls near,
It is also Canadian slang for a case of twenty-four beers.
The "two-fours" typically are popular during this holiday weekend.
When many Canadians get together with friends.

Like American long weekend celebrations of Memorial Day,
Canadians usher in long-awaited spring and an ensuing summer on
    this holiday.
After months of cold weather and an abundance of snow,
Northern skiers and skaters look forward to the sun aglow.

In 2020 will Canadians' holiday barbecues and parties be deferred
    due to COVID-19 fear?
How many will open trailers and cabins to get out summer gear?
Canadians may wonder whether there is truth to what they hear,
Will there be "cancellation" of summer they hold so dear?

Canada, a nation of 37 million people, has been hit by COVID-19.
Reports of 78,000+ cases and 5800+ deaths have been seen.
For our northern neighbor's sake, we hope the worst is in the past.
Yet, questions remain as to whether another wave of a COVID-19
    spell will be cast.

Will summer festivals like Toronto's popular Caribana still run?
For 50+ years, Canadians enjoyed this event filled with fun.
No Calgary Stampede, no Canadian National Exhibition in
    Toronto this year?
British Columbia cancelled sporting events, festivals, and concerts
    before the dates drew near.

Like those in the USA, holidays like Victoria Day will be marked
    in some way.
Summer festivities may change their configurations or be
    held at bay.
The pandemic of 2020 has made it abundantly clear,
Revisions occur daily to the symbols of culture and customs we
    hold so dear.

MEMORIAL DAY

May 25, 2020

Memorial Day is a holiday celebrated in the USA.
We observe this day on the last Monday in May,
To honor men and women in the armed forces who lost their lives
    in a military foray.
The commemoration originated in 1868 and was then named
    Decoration Day.

Decorating the graves of those who died defending our country
    became a tradition.
At its inception, this holiday honored deaths in the Civil War
    coalitions.
After World War I it paid tribute to members of our military who
    died by any war's definition.
A federal holiday in 1971, parades, celebrations, and memorials
    comprised many an exhibition.

We mourn our loved ones who lost lives in World War I, World
    War II, and Korea,
How many families sobbed through services mouthing words to
    the music of Ave Maria?
In the more recent conflicts of Iraq, Afghanistan, and Vietnam
    memories do not freely fade,
The Vietnam War, itself, lasted two decades.

During the Vietnam War 58,000 American lives were lost.
Many asked whether this sacrifice was worth the cost.
Wars, by their nature, bring conflict, uncertainty, and sacrifice.
Facing the enemy is not something easily enticed.

We'll honor those who died for us on this Memorial Day 2020,
However, the manner in which we do so may change for many.
Time honored traditions collide with increasingly new ways of life,
It is hard to know what to do or how to do it in times of strife.

Will we visit cemeteries and memorials to remember our brothers?
How many will join parades, parties, and barbecues with others?
On this Memorial Day 2020 we ourselves are engaged in a war.
A catastrophic enemy attacked us—an enemy we abhor.

In the U.S. 99,000+, in the world 348,000+, individuals have died
    within a mere few months,
The insidious COVID-19 seeks human bodies as it hunts.
These innocent victims died at the hands of the COVID-19 wrath,
1.6 million individuals in the U.S. and 5.5 million worldwide
        were in the COVID-19 path.

Some states, some countries have flattened the curve,
Others are just beginning to see COVID-19 swerve.
Staying home, social distancing, wearing masks continue,
Testing remains in the news at every venue.

We have been promised a vaccine by year end.
In the meantime, debates press on regarding the prophylactic
        merits of hydroxychloroquine.
"Travel bubbles" represents a phrase emerging in the news.
Speculation about "safe" places people can travel first, when
        tourism resumes.

As time goes by, life marches on in a unique and different way,
Humans are adaptable even when dismayed.
Some move fast, some move slow, trying to adjust,
Others choose "business as usual" as their thrust.

On this Memorial Day, the 25th of May,
We strive to remain purple despite a red and blue fray.
In this continuing pandemic, for our brothers and sisters who
        passed away,
For our doctors, nurses, hospital workers, and all service providers,
        we pray.

NUMBERS

May 27, 2020

Through words we express our thoughts.
We use idle words to talk, converse, discuss, chat, sometimes not
    really saying a lot.
A society must communicate, think, declare, decree, so by virtue of
    words we are taught.
We learn letters, sounds, usage, grammar, concepts, idioms, as we
    ought.

Words empower us to declare, guarantee, pledge, create poetry or
    prose with an interesting plot.
The Bible, Torah, Koran, Constitution, Shakespeare's sonnets—
    without words they'd be for not.
If we didn't express our feelings, emotions, pain, or pleasure in
    words, would we say we forgot?
Yet, there are times when words may be insufficient to relay the
    profound impact we sought.

Numbers convey information in penetrating, absolute stories of
    their own.
Today, May 27, provides an astonishing example now known.
We passed a mark, a way post, a landmark, a tragic milestone.
COVID-19 deaths in the USA entered an abominable zone.

These deaths--100,000+, occurred during a mere 12 weeks.
How do we assimilate or digest numbers reaching such peaks?
100,000 deaths in a mere 12 weeks.
100,000 deaths in a mere 12 weeks.

HUMBLE HEROES

May 29, 2020

What if we went to our mailboxes and found nothing there?
If we swirled our hands around in the boxes and found only air?
Does it matter not to have mail delivered each day?
Would we revert to obtaining post office boxes without delay?

What if the grocery store had no food on its shelves?
If we walked through the aisles and found no food-stocking elves?
Does it matter not to obtain every item during shopping delves?
Would we unload food transport trucks and stock shelves
    ourselves?

What if we learned that our local prison opened its doors?
If we no longer had prisoners in lockdown on prison floors?
Does it matter to approach criminal offenses with disregard?
Would we step in and volunteer to serve as prison guards?

What if parents or grandparents reside in a nursing home's hands?
If we no one bathed them or changed their bed pans?
Does it matter not to have our loved ones receive necessary care?
Would we attend to such needs if nurses' assistants were not there?

What if our neighbors contracted COVID-19 and their bodies
    needed to be transported?
If we no one moved the sick to the hospital and all efforts
    were thwarted?
Does it matter not to transfer sick bodies unescorted?
Would we appear masked and gloved so comported?

In 2020 the words "people matter" become increasingly trite.
Who will volunteer to become a mail deliverer, a grocery store
    food stocker, a prison guard, a nursing assistant, or an EMT
    tonight?
To all of these workers we owe a deep debt of gratitude.
They are our humble heroes of monumental magnitude.

THE TIME IS NOW

June 1, 2020

As the novel Coronavirus persisted in its hunts,
Our days melted into weeks and our weeks morphed into months.
COVID-19 casualties continued to climb.
On June 1, 2020 we note 1.7million cases, 104,000+ deaths in the
    USA and 6.2 million cases, 372,000+ deaths worldwide.

Many U.S. restaurants employed social distancing or table service
    outside.
However, some prospective customers were afraid to abide,
Questioning ample testing since so many have died.
If restaurants social distance, will their businesses reap
    sufficient profits to survive?

There are people who by their nature are carefree.
They don't take the pandemic seriously.
We have read stories about people hoarding TP,
And reports of swastika-armed protesters exhorting businesses to
    open on the basis of perceived personal liberty.

Amidst the pandemic's rampage other turmoil and tremors brew,
Protests in Minneapolis and dozens of other cities, reminiscent of
    1960s unrest we once knew.
The protests started out peaceful stressing grief, sorrow, hurt, and
    anger about issues.
Some turned to riots, looting, fires, and destruction too.

Protesters want their voices to be heard, not ignored, as they feel
    they have been hitherto.
Officials say they understand but need to restore order by calling in
    reserves and setting curfews.
Mayors indicate the protests were peaceful until outsiders
    turned nonviolent protests askew.
Are outsiders with separate agendas involved? To date we don't
    know what is true.

We see a country in chaos with festering problems long overdue.
COVID-19, along with precarious crises, could cause our country
    to come unglued.
40 million have filed unemployment claims as job loss grew.
Eviction moratoriums expire in cities as monthly bills accrue.

Lines in food pantries grow and domestic violence is on the rise,
Our economy may be shattered which is no surprise.
One day's news cycle debates social media being muzzled or
    how school should resume,
The next day it's the legality of voting by mail, or college
    classes on Zoom.

Every challenge brings an opportunity—yes, this sounds trite.
But what are our choices we ask outright?
Where are our leaders? Is our country going to fall apart?
Can we pull ourselves together and restart?

We can think about folks singing from their balconies on high,
Citizens sewing masks and medical workers risking their lives.
It is difficult to balance First Amendment rights, protests, riots, and
    masses who disagree.
Our country survived a revolution, a civil war, two world wars,
    assassinations, 9/11 and we're still free.

The USA has the world's top technology companies leading
    us to and through
Artificial intelligence, autonomous vehicles, cloud computing,
    drones, and other possibilities too.
Our dollar is the world's main reserve currency.
The US has surging oil production and exemplary food producing
    capacity.

In this chaotic time, do we not have a serious mandate to use
    our capability?
To learn from the pandemic and its chaotic calamities,
To meet worldly challenges and create opportunities,
To apply intellectual and financial capital to operate differently.

Living through a pandemic may assure us we can develop
individual self-sufficiency.
Can we also govern ourselves, while gaining pandemic prevention
proficiency?
Can we improve pandemic supply chain management efficiency?
Can we increase innovation for fighting future pandemics, while
decreasing our deficiencies?

Can we put our heads together and address lingering deep-rooted
problems in our society?
The time is now.

D-DAY

June 6, 2020

On June 6, 2020 we celebrate the anniversary of D-Day, also
    known as Operation Overlord.
It signifies the day a World War II battle began on June 6, 1944.
During the Battle of Normandy, 156,000 American, British, and
    Canadian forces
Landed on five Normandy beaches, with their might and
    amphibious military assault resources.

By August 1944 the Allies' efforts resulted in Western Europe's
    liberation
From Nazi Germany's control and domination.
By the following spring, the Allies had defeated the enemy nation.
The beginning of the end of war in Europe is marked by Normandy
    landings, without hesitation.

Decades passed since World War II began in 1939, ending in 1945.
The world now has an invisible predatory enemy insidiously alive.
In the USA to date there have been 1.9 million COVID-19 cases
    and 109,000+ have died.
Across America protests continued, more voices decried.

COVID-19 and pandemic preparedness had dominated the news
    cycle week after week,
Until George Floyd's death, when protests of police brutality
    started to leak.
Our beloved America's divisions once again came into full view.
Instead of one priority battle we now have two.

Despite the risks of COVID-19, protests in countries and cities
    around the world emerged.
In Australia, Japan, Sweden, Zimbabwe, Paris, London, Berlin,
    support for George Floyd surged.
On D-Day 2020 we ask when and how we will unearth the
    beginning of the end
Of these two wars, from which we, as a nation, desperately need to
    ascend.

THE FIRST DAY OF SUMMER

June 20, 2020

To everything in life, is there a season?
A time, a purpose, or a reason?
Do life's experiences, like threads in a tapestry, interweave,
So that a back view looks confusing while the front view illustrates
    what we believe?

Is the current era a time to grieve?
For the 2.2 million people in the USA who suffered or the nearly
    120,000 pandemic deaths we bereave.
Are we missing a message from this epic pandemic, the
    existence of which we want to disbelieve?
Why did so many have to die? From these deaths, what meaning
    do we perceive?

Are we also entering a season when we come to terms with
    systemic racism many aggrieve?
As a nation we have experienced weeks of protests, by people of
    all colors, without reprieve.
What is the message we take away from the protesters and what
    they are trying to achieve?
Is this the time for the world to examine what is before our eyes,
    yet often difficult to conceive?

Spring is long gone when June 20 marks the first day of summer.
Daffodils and crocuses are now replaced by sunflowers, zinnias,
    and other heat tolerant newcomers.
As summer approaches, via travel by plane, train, boat, bus, or car,
Typically, people head for beaches, mountains, sightseeing, near
    and far.

During the summer months of 2020, how many people will remain
    in quarantine,
As worldwide cases climb to 8.6 million and deaths to 460,000+
    due to COVID-19?
Under the heavens, alluring sunshine, blue skies, and hot summer
    days aglow,
Entice us to become complacent about the virulent virus we know.

Or to forget about the recent deaths of black men, from which
    summer may enable us to cleave,
As news cycles change and sunshine removes the shadows from
    souls who once were naïve.
The splendor of summer is a blessing from above, a divine gift, a
    welcome present we receive.
Let us pray summer bliss doesn't blind us to messages we were
    meant to retrieve.

To everything in life, is there a season?
A time, or a purpose, or a reason?
Do life's experiences, like threads in a tapestry, interweave,
So that a back view looks confusing while the front view illustrates
    what we believe?

FATHER'S DAY

June 21, 2020

Today, June 21, 2020 is Father's Day,
A day we honor our fathers—those with us and those who have
    passed away.
In Spokane, Washington the country's first Father's Day occurred
    on June 19, 1910.
Five years later, President Wilson used telegraph signals to
    remotely unfurl a Father's Day flag in Spokane.

In 1924 President Coolidge appealed to state governments to
    promote the holiday again.
And, in the 1920s and 1930s groups attempted to establish a
    Parent's Day, instead of a separate day to honor women and
    another to honor men.
Yet, the holiday survived the Great Depression and World War II.
Advertisers, as well as sentimentalists, espoused the day as an
    institution through and through.

In 1972 President Nixon proclaimed Father's Day a federal holiday
    with the stroke of a pen.
We have been honoring our fathers in the USA on the third Sunday
    of June since then.
Some other countries honor their fathers on St. Joseph's Day
    which falls on March 19.
Europe and Latin America choose this Catholic holiday to honor
    fathers as is their routine.

How will Father's Day be celebrated in 2020 during a global
    pandemic and social unrest?
How will we tell our fathers how much they mean to us and that, in
    our eyes, they are the best?
How many families will social distance and wear masks during
    Father's Day visits?
How many will go to restaurants to enjoy favorite meals so
    exquisite?

How many of the 2,260,000+ who have suffered from COVID-19
    have been fathers?
How many of the 119,700+ who died were dads passing away
    alone, feeling desperation or fearing no one bothers?
How many children lost their papas due to COVID-19?
How many kids lost their daddies to other crises in our country
    before anyone could intervene?

Let's tell our fathers, our mothers, our sisters, our brothers, our
    children and our friends,
How much they mean to us before another day ends.

FOURTH OF JULY

July 4, 2020

On the Fourth of July we celebrate Independence Day,
Commemorating the Continental Congress voting independence
    from Britain for the USA.
On July 2, 1776 this decision involved much consternation
    and deliberation,
As well as hesitation, cogitation, and mediation.

July 4, 1776, 13 colonies adopted our Declaration of Independence
    denoting our country's birth.
Since then we celebrate this day with fireworks, parades, concerts,
    picnics, and much mirth.
Thomas Jefferson drafted the declaration delineating how much
    our independence was worth.
From that day forward, through times of joy and times of sorrow,
    our country grew to be exemplary on God's earth.

After the War of 1812 when the USA again faced Great Britain in
    another historic fix,
The holiday remained, never to be nixed,
America celebrated fifty years of independence on July 4, 1826.
This same day, two former presidents, Thomas Jefferson and John
    Adams, were sick.

Who could have predicted the two founding fathers would die on
    the same day in the same year?
And, that this memorable day would be July 4, 1826, a holiday to
    their hearts so dear.
Five years later on this very same July 4th holiday,
Our fifth president, and founder, James Monroe, passed away.

In 1870, Congress's efforts to make July 4th a federal holiday kept
    Independence Day alive.
Decades passed and it continued to thrive.
In 1941 to federal employees a paid July 4th holiday the
    government would provide.
Citizens continued to celebrate Independence Day each year until
    the day entered our archives.

July 4th became an integral microcosm of the fabric of our nation,
A translation of our history that survives despite reverberation,
A respite from the daily routine to enjoy a long weekend or a
    summer vacation,
A time to barbecue with friends, family, and relations.

July 4, 2020 marks a midpoint through a tumultuous six months,
A time many may not choose to experience more than once.
To some, social distancing, masks, sanitizer are part of the past.
To others they are critical so COVID-19 does not remain steadfast.

Some shun science, declaring a fiasco blown out of proportion.
Others decry science to guide us to clarity without distortion.
Are facts being twisted and turned into contortions?
Or are "alternate facts" being apportioned to our misfortune?

Of somethings we can be sure.
Excessive division in our country expands even more.
Citizens disconnect from each other from shore to shore,
Until ultimately, as a people, we are rocked to our core.

The USA, a country once thought to be "exceptional,"
Will it dither away far from founding fathers' intent, so original?
There are 2.8 million COVID-19 cases in the USA, those in the
    south and west rising fast.
Yet, individuals defy science by purporting the pandemic is past.

The European Union managed the virus with positive results.
The EU now opens its borders for tourism, but travel from the
     U.S., the EU halts.
USA accounts for 4% of world population but close to 25% of the
     world's 11 million COVID-19 cases.
Consequently, the EU looks at the USA while it stalls and braces.

EU's 27 countries with population of nearly 450 million fought
     COVID-19 with skill and might,
To control the COVID-19 spread, while USA's 50,000+ case
     counts reach new heights.
Where did we go wrong and how do we make it right?
Medical experts tell us, we cannot contain this rate
     of disease spread without consistent, clear messaging and
     discipline in our fight.

Doctors Without Borders, an international medical humanitarian
     non-governmental organization
In over 70 countries, treats people threatened by violence,
     disasters, emergencies, and depravation.
Are we surprised to learn Doctors Without Borders COVID-19
     response teams' dedication
Provides support to vulnerable communities lacking access to
     resources in our very own nation?

While the pandemic raged, the U.S. Supreme Court brought clarity
     to sex discrimination in June.
The Court told Dreamers it's ok to remain in the U.S. for the time
     being, at least a trial balloon,
And, that detained children in ICE detention centers can go back to
     family members soon.
As 129,000+ U.S. pandemic deaths mounted, debates about statues
     and monuments were hewn.

Meanwhile, we hear about bounties placed on our military's heads
by a foreign government.
If so, who knew, what did they know, and when will the truth of
this matter be apparent?
An unemployment rate of 11.1%, down from 14.7% in April, may
sound like good news,
But it remains a higher unemployment rate than previous periods
since World War II.

Growing pandemic, precarious economic outlook, social unrest,
bounties—dilemmas compound.
To outsiders our country resembles a rudderless vessel circling
around and around.
Will tanker, *America*, drift further into the deep? Could it
eventually hit shoals and go aground?
Or will *America* be rescued by its citizens who reflect on July 4th
and together resound?

SOUTH AMERICA'S PANDEMIC

July 8, 2020

How are our friends in South America faring during COVID-19?
Some countries are holding their own and others' results could
　　have been foreseen.
South America is the fourth largest continent in the world,
With 12 countries and three territories, 6.9 million square miles for
　　COVID-19 to be unfurled.

Brazil has 212 million people and is also the largest country on the
　　South American continent.
Known for its 118-foot-tall Christ the Redeemer monument,
Built on a 2310-foot summit on Mount Corcovado, visible from
　　anywhere in Rio de Janeiro,
The monument had been lit up with world flags of COVID-19
　　countries across the globe.

In Brazil where the bulk of the world's largest rainforest exists, the
　　COVID-19 threat grew.
National parks were ordered closed, including the one featuring the
　　flags and the Christ statue.
Brazil now leads South America in the number of COVID-19 cases
　　and in deaths too,
1.6 million cases and 66,000+ deaths—second only to the case
　　counts the USA has accrued.

On July 7, 2020 it was reported that Jair Bolsonaro, Brazil's 38th
　　president,
Who in the past downplayed the threat of COVID-19 to
　　Brazil's residents,
Tested positive for the virus, most likely a recent discovery.
The world will be watching the stages of the 65-year old
　　president's recovery.

Brazil is reported to be on the forefront of large-scale trials and
   possibly vaccine development.
Oxford University in partnership with AstraZeneca labs report
   vaccine movement.
Also, China's Sinovac relays another similarly advanced vaccine
   improvement.
Phase Three clinical tests—the last before approval—are to be
   carried out on Brazil's residents.

While Brazil's lockdown measures may not have been applied
   effectively in that nation,
The country may benefit from technology transfer agreements to
   avoid vaccine rations.
Under the agreements, Brazil could produce the vaccines
   themselves—an important key.
In the world to date only three vaccine projects have reached
   Phase Three.

Among a few other countries, Brazil may become a vaccine depot.
For Brazilians, as well as other Latin Americans, this possibility
   may open a bright window.
Large scale clinical trials like these bring hope to the world like
   gold at the end of a rainbow.
For vaccine programs let us pray to Christ the Redeemer
   monument on Mount Corcovado.

Peru was one of the first countries in the region imposing
   lockdown to curb COVID-19.
Challenges affected the enforcement, the population, and disturbed
   lives and their routines.
President Martin Vizcarra described the crisis as the "most
   serious" in the country's history.
To this country of 32 million, like many others in the world, the
   virus remains a mystery.

Reports of 309,000+ cases and nearly 11,000 deaths surface in
    Peru.
Second highest case counts in South America after Brazil, the
    reports are troublesome to view.
Once known for its strong economy, Peru has millions out of work
    and a sick economy too.
This year Peru will not be hosting many trips to its 15th century
    Inca site, Machu Picchu.

Chile's President Sebastian Pinera proposed $1.5 billion stimulus
    package not a minute too soon.
It followed a jump in unemployment to 11% and a $12 billion
    stimulus package in June.
For Chile's 19 million people, the COVID-19 virus is hitting the
    struggling middle class hard,
301,000+ cases and 6400+ deaths keep the country on guard.

Columbia with 50 million people, 124,000+ cases, and 4600+
    deaths, was to open on July 15.
President Ivan Duque now says national lockdown will extend
    until Aug. 1 due to COVID-19.
During the pandemic Columbia, Latin America's fourth largest
    economy, has been shattered.
Employment, business closures, and a top export--crude oil, has
    been battered.

Argentina with a population of 45 million has 83,000+ cases
    and 1600+ have died.
The tango, Patagonia, Iguazu Falls, Mendoza wineries, Recoleta
    Cemetery where Evita resides,
Are now only past memories for tourists, like the Bariloche
    sunrise.
President Alberto Fernandez toughened lockdown in Buenos Aires
    due to COVID-19 case size.

Ecuador's third deputy working on the pandemic reportedly
    recently resigned.
In a country with population of 17 million and 63,000+ cases,
    4800+ have died.
Guayaquil suffered one of Latin America's worst COVID-19
    outbreaks in April and March.
Due to strains in hospital capacity, victims' bodies were left in
    homes and streets, parched.

Bolivia, a country of 11 million with poverty, unrest, and strife,
Has suffered to date with 41,000+ COVID-19 cases, 1500+ of
    which experienced loss of life.
Cochabamba, in the center of Bolivia, was one of the hardest hit
    areas in the nation.
It has been overwhelmed by COVID-19 as many bodies pile up
    awaiting burial or cremation.

For months, **Venezuela**, a country of 28 million has been under
    quarantine.
To date it has reported, if accurate, 7600+ cases and 71 deaths due
    to COVID-19.
Medical personnel report a lack of PPE in the OPEC country
    struggling with hyperinflation,
An economic crisis that weakens basic services like running water
    and hospital sanitation.

Today, to **Uruguay**, a progressive country, it is reported the UAE
    sent 7 metric tons of medical supplies.
Uruguay uses special teams to test random city blocks and critical
    job sectors besides.
Results in this country of 3 million are reported successful with
    960+ cases and 29 died.
However, reportedly, of most concern is the border with Brazil
    where COVID-19's net is wide.

Paraguay, a poor, landlocked country of 7 million seems to
control COVID-19.
Despite high poverty and poor public health, Paraguay closed its
borders, imposing quarantine.
The country built two public hospitals to deal with a possible surge
in cases.
With only 2500+ reported cases and 20 deaths, Paraguay's main
concern is the case count in Brazil, as it races.

Long term concern in Paraguay and countries nearby is the drop in
GDP for economies already weak,
And, public health care systems unprepared for how much havoc a
major epidemic would wreak,
For smaller countries like **Guyana** and **Suriname** there is not
much information to be untied.
The former's 786,000+ people have 284 cases, the latter's
population of 586,000+ has 634 cases and in both countries,
due to COVID-19, 16 and 15 people, respectively, have died.

In the USA today COVID-19 cases mounted to 3 million with
131,000+ deaths.
These rising case counts cause us concern as we hold our breath.
And, the world's case count has reached 12 million with deaths
of 545,000 or more.
Let us pray for our country and for nations in our world from shore
to shore.

BASTILLE DAY

July 14, 2020

Commemorated on July 14 each year, Bastille Day is the national
    day of France.
The anniversary of two historic dates, French National Day does
    advance:
The Storming of the Bastille on July 14, 1789, noted as a turning
    point in the French Revolution,
And July 14, 1790, *Fete de la Fédération,* celebrates unity of
    French people, an evolution.

The oldest and largest regularly held military parade in Europe is
    held on *le 14 juillet,*
In front of the President of the Republic on Paris's
    Champs-Elysées.
French officials and foreign guests attend.
French citizens celebrate with their relatives and friends.

Bastille Day is revered in other parts of the world.
In Belgium, Canada, Czech Republic, Hungary, New Zealand,
    South Africa, the UK, regions of the USA, and other countries,
    remembrances are unfurled.
Merry making includes French food, games, music, songs,
    concerts, street actors who perform.
Before the jubilation ends, fireworks and balls are the norm.

In 2020, French President Emmanuel Macron focuses on recovery
    of France from COVID-19,
By tackling the social and economic results of the pandemic while
    making changes to his team.
His priorities center on unemployment, jobs, the disenfranchised,
    and an economy that is green.
He promotes EU adoption of a large stimulus package to help the
    bloc recover as it reconvenes.

We wish our 65 million French brothers and sisters well as they
    manage COVID-19's fate.
France has 199,000+ of the world's 12.9 million cases and
    29,000+ of 570,000+ deaths to date.
However, the country's new case count has diminished to a
    promising low rate.
In the USA, we strive for lower cases counts we could more
    comfortably navigate.

With 3.4 million cases and 136,000+ deaths, containment is now
    USA's primary goal.
Medical experts tell us that too much community spread may make
    contact tracing futile.
Since USA action plans are left to the states, how will each state
    get its cases under control?
Mask mandating rests with states, counties, cities, or with each
    individual soul.

Without a national strategic pandemic plan in the USA, many
    citizens fear for our fate.
Precious hours of daily life feature cable news coverage of topics
    given constant media weight.
Themes focus on COVID-19, public health, social unrest, the
    economy, now all subjects of debate.
Others hone in on division, discord, dissension, dissonance,
    disunion, and hate.

Are hospitals in some states running out of ICU space due to this
    dreadful virus today?
Or are 99% of COVID-19 cases harmless, as some say?
Are people growing numb to the increase in COVID-19
    cases and deaths?
Why are we still not clear about whether our country has enough
    tests?

Health officials advise avoiding large groups in any shape or form.
Will conventions occur in 2020 where thousands could be
    exposed as COVID-19 swarms?
Colleges and universities continue to grapple with how to hold
    classes in the fall.
Will foreign students be banned from attending classes at all?

Whether children return to school during the next weeks or months
    rages into a stalemate.
Who makes decisions? Is a new federal power replacing the law of
    each state?
We want to make good decisions for our children so they can
    continue to learn,
But won't we need uniform policies and protocols for masking to
    alleviate parents' concerns?

How will children, in their classrooms, be social distanced within
    six feet?
Shouldn't all stakeholders--parents, teachers, school
    administrators, unions, legislators meet?
Will expertise, knowledge, issues, concerns, contentions, questions
    be placed on the table?
Won't funding be required so that children's socially distanced
    learning can be stable?

How exactly will federal funding be withheld if states and
    municipalities do not comply?
The Center for Disease Control set forth guidelines for school re-
    opening, don't they apply?
Why is there so much confusion about this issue when other
    countries have done so effectively?
Is this an issue of safety, public health, education, economics, or
    will it be handled politically?

Mexico now bars US citizens from crossing its borders.
Who could have predicted COVID-19 would result in this policy
    reversal in short order?

President Andres Manuel Lopez Obrador of Mexico, flying coach,
    made his way to the USA.
Why didn't Canada's Justin Trudeau show up for this meeting
    day?

Why are Confederate flags such a hot topic in the USA?
Is Bubba Wallace's experience a hate crime or a hoax, as some
    portray?
What happened to hundreds of children separated from families at
    the border two years ago?
Have they been returned to family members, does anyone know?

Has a foreign government placed bounties on the heads of our
    military in Afghanistan?
Why can't the public get a clear response to this question in a
    reasonable time span?
Will there be objective investigations and eventually a long-
    awaited rebuke?
Or will we, on Bastille Day, be told this matter is just another
    fluke?

The U.S. Supreme Court ruled that states can force their electors to
    vote as agreed.
Will delegates still try to "undue" the electoral college after
    commitments have been decreed?
On July7, 2020 the USA took the first official step in the process to
    withdraw from the WHO.
In the midst of a pandemic why would the USA do so?

Why do the same questions seem to float week after week?
Why are there so many diversions, digressions, deflections, and
    pivots to the answers we seek?
Will the USA reach a turning point in its COVID-19 war and its
    culture revolutions?
Will US citizens have their own "Bastille-like Day" and celebrate
    their unity as an American people, without retribution?

TESTING, TESTING, TESTING

July 20, 2020

Testing, testing, testing—cacophony ringing in each ear,
Testing, testing, testing—information confounding what we read
    and hear,
Testing, testing, testing—myths encircling like a discombobulated
    sphere,
Testing, testing, testing—steps for alleviating public fear.

Initially citizens were told the USA needed more COVID-19 tests.
The USA didn't adopt those of the WHO, believing its own would
    be best.
Experts scrambled posthaste to develop COVID-19 tests during
    periods subsequently compressed.
Yet, as the COVID-19 case counts rose, demand for tests had not
    been addressed.

Bumbling words pour out as we try to ascertain truth regarding
    what is being expressed.
After months of the pandemic, why so many long lines for those
    awaiting a COVID-19 test?
Contemporaneously, "anyone can get a test," public officials attest.
Up and down, back and forth, testing myths and facts, truths and
    untruths, are professed.

Next it was purported the tests aren't the problem, more swabs
    and reagents we need to request.
And then we hear there aren't enough licensed labs—that is why
    testing gets repressed.
As we try to keep apprised of pandemic news, testing remains a
    question people contest.
On July 20 we learn *testing* may not be the issue—the problem
    rests with tests being *processed*.

Why can some COVID-19 tests be processed in an hour or less?
Why are other COVID-19 tests requiring processing time of more
    than two weeks at best?
If it takes so long to get a test result, how does that help
    COVID-19 from being suppressed?
While awaiting days or weeks for test results, how much spread of
    virus remains unaddressed?

Regarding our 3 million cases and 140,000+ deaths, many are
    profoundly depressed.
One way to lower those number in the USA--an easy solution
    others suggest,
Just reduce the testing! The resulting number of COVID-19 cases
    will be compressed.
Is this counterintuitive to the effect of positivity rates, or an
    attempt to erase pandemic distress?

Why do other developed countries master testing without suffering
    domestic unrest?
Why does the USA, once a world leader in such matters, remain
    repressed?
Instead of circuitously debating issues in rhetorical modes or
    political quests,
Why can't the USA use its intellectual assets to develop
    "on-the-spot" COVID-19 tests?

Isn't this the technology for brainpower and funders to invest?
Talk is cheap, so the trite expression will attest.
Unfettered expert action can still be manifest.
Before it is too late, let's pray the USA's red and blue divisions
    around these issues coalesce.

MASKS

July 21, 2020

During this pandemic why is the wearing of masks such a big deal?
Does mandating masks violate constitutional rights, causing
    personal pain that can't heal?
How is public safety to be balanced with individual liberty during
    a pandemic so real?
Are masks intended to protect the wearer? Or their sisters and
    brothers?
Is the topic of masks "all about me," or for public health safety and
    consideration of others?

One way to approach the masking debate,
Is to walk in the shoes of victims' loved ones before it's too late.

Let us walk in the shoes of:
A wife who says goodbye to her husband on an ambulance gurney
    never to see him alive again,
A teenager whose classmate died from COVID-19 and lost
    his friend,
A husband whose wife, an ER nurse, fought COVID-19 to the end,
A daughter whose father, in isolation on a ventilator, sobbed for
    words of love she couldn't send,
A military son whose mother contracted COVID-19 and words of
    prayer to her could only be penned,
A girl whose young, healthy, physically fit fiancé died from
    COVID-19, her only boyfriend,
A boy who watched both parents suffer from COVID-19 and after
    they died his heart will not mend,
A parent who loses a child to COVID-19, at any age a death
    difficult to comprehend,
A colleague who tends to a revered doctor with COVID-19 upon
    whom others used to depend,
A student whose beloved teacher died of COVID-19 before the
    weekend,
A doctor who cries as a patient dies, despite the care he did extend.

During this pandemic why is the wearing of masks such a big deal?
Can we take into account the health and safety of others when we
    make this appeal?
Let's come together and put the facts on the table and not conceal,
The depth of suffering in our nation is real.
Let's not be afraid of what our actions may reveal.

HUMILITY AND HUMANITY

July 27, 2020

Amidst a nation in disarray, we mourn the passing of John Lewis
    during tributes today.
At age 80, he left us on July 17, 2020 after battling Stage 4
    pancreatic cancer, an insidious fray.
We won't forget the distinctive voice of the
    Congressman on the House floor,
A member of the House of Representatives from Georgia,
    but so much more.

To sharecroppers in rural Alabama on February 21, 1940 he was
    born.
From our memories, shocking images of his beating in Selma, will
    never be shorn.
It was always nonviolence that this Civil Rights icon espoused,
    exemplified, and forewarned.
As one of the original 13 Freedom Riders, from his moral authority
    he would not be torn.

John Lewis founded and led the Student Nonviolent Coordinating
    Committee--SNCC,
An organization coordinating lunch-counter sit-ins when tensions
    were thick.
He fought for racial justice, equality, and human rights so that all
    might someday be free.
John Lewis helped organize the March on Washington where
    Dr. King spoke in 1963.

Mr. Lewis was brave, courageous, stalwart, undaunted, and bold.
While leading demonstrations against segregated restrooms,
    restaurants, and hotels, he experienced bloody beatings, a
    fractured skull, being spat upon, and suffering untold.
Lewis led one of the most famous marches in American history on
    March 7, 1965,
Marching across the Edmund Pettus Bridge in Selma for voting
    rights that had been denied.

When U.S. citizens woke up to see beatings of Mr. Lewis and
    others on their TV news,
They became outraged at the brutality, deciding to support the
    Voting Rights Act, long overdue.
LBJ signed the Voting Rights Act of 1965 whereby blacks secured
    the right to vote.
Literacy tests were struck down as a requisite to voter registration
    with restrictions to note.

During decades of dedicated service in the House of
    Representatives, Lewis rarely showed stress.
He was known as the conscience of the U.S. Congress.
Despite a hectic schedule, when asked if he had a few minutes to
    chat, he always said yes.
Causes of human rights or people in distress, he doggedly tried to
    address.

No matter what he achieved, he remained a humble man.
A kind, empathetic mentor to many, he is known for his
    willingness to lend a helping hand.
Such humility and humanity he bequeathed to those of us who
    remain.
During the pandemic, economic crisis, and social unrest of 2020,
    emulating John Lewis provides us a path to follow on a
    challenging terrain.

INTERESTING TIMES

August 3, 2020

For many the monotony of the pandemic has become routine.
Seven months of 2020 have passed and our country continues to
    struggle with COVID-19.
We have had 4.6 million COVID cases in the USA and 155,000+
    souls have died.
Some citizens characterize the pandemic as a hoax, while
    others take the updates in stride.

It is reported that vaccine Phase III trials from University of
    Oxford and Moderna are underway.
Other efficacy trials seem to start every day.
Healthy adult volunteers receiving vaccine or placebos will be
    monitored for side effects and tested for infection.
It is hoped that at the end of the trial 70% of those vaccinated
    would receive COVID-19 protection.

But what if less efficacy is met?
Is it better to manufacture a weak vaccine or keep trying for one
    with higher efficacy to vet?
Scientists report optimism for the development of a vaccine.
Timing to obtain efficacy and manufacturing remains to be seen.

Meanwhile, whether to open schools, citizens discuss in despair.
In the domain of local school boards rests students' and teachers'
    welfare.
Public health and safety, educational principles, budgets, day care
    needs, sports, all go into the hornet's nest.
Parents, teachers, students feel strongly about what they perceive
    to be best.

At the same time, clouds over the economy loom,
Q2's unemployment rate is noted at 11.1%--a sign of gloom.
Real GDP decreased at an annual rate of 32.9 % in Q2,
Experts indicate, until the pandemic case counts decrease, there is
    little we can do.

As these topics swirl in the news, public figures' soundbites
    get intoned,
It has been suggested the general election in November be
    postponed.
Do we postpone general elections in the USA?
Why would we consider proceeding this way?

Those who appreciate history or are inclined to read,
Recall the Constitution gives Congress the power to choose
    timing of general elections--a founding fathers' creed.
Federal law enacted in 1845 set dates for general elections as the
    first Tuesday after the first Monday in November.
To change this law requires new legislation approved by the
    House, the Senate, and the President—lest we misremember.

In this time of the pandemic our heads get cloggy and it is easy to
    forget.
Didn't we have an election during the Civil War, WWI, WWII,
    and the 1918 flu pandemic without much fret?
Since we are in a pandemic, some have suggested voting by mail
    to prevent risk of going to the polls.
Surely the USA has the technology and the know-how to do so
    with proper controls, while forestalling trolls.

There is also discussion of voter fraud being a national scare.
Aren't there a number of studies showing any type of voter
    fraud is rare?
Wasn't there a presidential investigation into election corruption
    that was disbanded in 2018 due to no finding of fraud?
Shouldn't officials address voting by mail posthaste to
    assure secure voting, health and safety of citizenry? Does *not*
    doing so seem odd?

We have experienced other summers, compared to 2020, that
    would now seem sublime.
As Confucius once stated, "may you live in interesting times."

THE UNITED STATES POSTAL SERVICE

August 16, 2020

The U.S. postal service was established by the Second Continental
    Congress on July 26, 1775.
Benjamin Franklin served as the country's first Postmaster General
    and kept it alive.
Franklin's service with the mail system had its own unique history,
Despite his relationship with the British which could be blistery.

In 1753, Benjamin Franklin, who had served as postmaster of
    Philadelphia in prior days,
Became one of two joint postmasters general for our 13 colonies,
    instituting new ways
For improving the mail system and halting delays.
Franklin knew how to study operations and practices he needed to
    appraise.

Franklin set up revised, more efficient colonial postal routes.
Mail delivery was cut in half between Philadelphia and New York
    through ingenious pursuits,
Utilizing weekly mail wagon relay teams traveling day and night,
    Franklin was quite astute.
Franklin implemented procedures in his typical manner—
    emphatically resolute.

Benjamin Franklin standardized mail delivery costs by establishing
    the first chart for mail rates.
Based on, then, new concepts, like distance and weight.
In 1774 Benjamin Franklin was fired from his job as postmaster
    because of his revolutionary activities.
However, being fired did not diminish Franklin's proclivities.

In 1775 he was appointed Postmaster General of the United
  Colonies by the Continental Congress, a position he held until
  1776 when he went to France as a diplomat.
His postal system legacy included postal routes from Maine to
  Florida and service between the colonies and Britain—the
  country was proud of that.
In 1789 President George Washington appointed a former
  congressman, Samuel Osgood, as the first Postmaster General
  of the USA.
At that time there were 75 post offices in the country, rising to
  nearly 40,000 post offices today.

Our post offices deliver 212 billion pieces of mail per year.
Mail travels to 144 million homes and businesses in the USA and
  its territories so dear.
The postal service delivers our letters, cards, packages, medicines,
  and more,
Rain or shine to our front doors.

In 2020, during the COVID-19 pandemic our postal service
  has come under attack.
Is the reasoning behind this intervention to get costs and efficiency
  on track?
Why do many citizens view an American icon being diminished
  and want their postal service back?
Why are various mail sorting machines purportedly being removed
  from post offices despite the flack?

Why are some states involved in litigation concerning the U.S.
  Postal Service?
A number of citizens say that changes to the postal service are
  making them nervous.
If postal rules change, how will retirees receive their Medicare
  benefits on time?
Will veterans be at risk if arrival of their prescription
  medications is obstructed as delays begin to climb?

Narratives of postal slowdowns and reduced services sound off
like drumbeats across the nation.
During an election year and a pandemic what is the purpose of
such an endeavor's fixation?
Shouldn't our leaders return from their recess to address the root of
this dilemma's causation?
In the year 2020 does the United States need yet another crisis and
machination?

100th ANNIVERSARY OF WOMEN'S SUFFRAGE AND THE RIGHT TO VOTE

August 18, 2020

This month marks the anniversary of historical events
    unprecedented in a prodigious way.
Today 68 million women vote in elections as a result of the 19th
    Amendment in the USA.
The first women's rights convention was held in Seneca Falls,
    New York in 1848.
For the next 72 years women lobbied, protested, and marched,
    entering the public debate.

On May 21, 1919 the U.S. House of Representatives approved the
    Susan B. Anthony Amendment, guaranteeing for women the
    right to vote.
Within a few weeks the 19th Amendment went to the Senate where
    it continued to float.
Next, the 19th Amendment went to the then 48 states where it had
    to be ratified.
At least three-fourths of these states were needed in order for the
    Constitution to be satisfied.

On August 18, 1920, Tennessee cast its vote, making it the last
    state needed
To bring forth the 19th Amendment as its execution was heeded.
As of August 26, 1920, American women's right to vote would
    forever be protected.
By proclamation of the then Secretary of State, the 19th
    Amendment was ratified and effected.

Henceforth U.S. citizens could not be denied the right to vote on
    the basis of sex.
In many ways this amendment was seen as a way for women to
    clear the decks.
Women were finally equal in the USA.
Or were they?

Not to diminish the celebration of the 100-year anniversary of
    women's right to vote,
But questions loom in our historical memories we still note.
Why did it take so long for women to be granted this right?
Who held the women's rights advocates back for 72 years as they
    fought the good fight?

2020 also marks the 150th anniversary of passage of the 15th
    Amendment, another one upon which history takes note.
This milestone in U.S. history gave African Americans the
    right to vote.
Voting rights couldn't be denied "on account of race, color, or
    previous conditions of servitude."
Ratified on February 3, 1870, the 15th Amendment should have
    enabled African Americans to exude.

This year marks the anniversary of yet another milestone—the 50th
    anniversary of the Voting Rights Act Amendments of 1970,
Abolishing literacy tests, among other methods of disenfranchising
    voters, of which there were plenty.
In 2020 celebrating these legislative achievements in rapid
    succession creates an impression.
Does this mean that voting rights are clear cut and above board—
    no voter suppression?

Can voting rights be granted and then taken away?
Could this happen in a country like our beloved USA?
Many people might furrow their brows and say "no way!"
But what do we really know about how voting transpires today?

Some voting rules may look like sheep in wolves clothing as
    though wearing a disguise.
Methods are not always overt; consequently, confusion may result
    in discerning what underlies.
Fraud prevention, typically reasonable on its face, may be but a
    stated guise
For discriminatory purges of voter rolls, stripping registered voters
    of their status during "updates" certain states devise.

The pandemic of 2020 opens the door to additional potential for
      voter suppression.
Resisting the risk of going to the polls due to COVID-19, many
      people perceive mail-in voting to be a logical suggestion.
Wouldn't mail-in voting provide an opportunity to increase voter
      participation?
In America don't we want maximum participation in voting for the
      betterment of our nation?

Don't the states of Colorado, Hawaii, Oregon, Utah and
      Washington employ mail-in voting for all election sessions?
Haven't absentee ballots been used for years by states without
      transgression?
Why do some portray mail-in voting as "illegal" or try to create
      that impression?
Are promoters of this premise naïve or are they surreptitiously
      promoting voter repression?

It is important to dig deep under the facts when trying to
      discover truth or oppression.
On its face residency requirements appear to be reasonable as a
      requirement's expression.
But what do we know about the residences of Native Americans
      living on a reservation?
Are we aware that Native American reservations typically may not
      have streets with numbered homes at their discretion?

Some districts find ways to address these voter ID requirements by
      designating a polling place and similar intercessions.
Others have done so in form, but in substance continue aggression.
Minority voters have had to face various digressions.
Would we like our polling station to be a re-purposed feather-filled
      chicken coop preceded by voting lines in a multi-hour
      procession?

Consider going to the polls to meet poll workers with hands on
their guns—a true voting experience regression.
If we had to wait in line for five or six hours to vote while officials
stared at us, would we be met with a favorable impression?
Are such voting practices focused on the prevention of voter fraud?
Or are they a stand-in for a voter suppression squad?

What should we construe from shortened voting hours/days and
changes in polling places?
What about poll closures, misinformation, voting rule changes
without a basis?
How do we feel about onerous voter registration rules and
questionable voter purges?
Do any of these practices promote our precious right to vote and
voting surges?

Some countries, like Australia, have a mandatory right to vote.
Despite COVID-19 can the USA rise to the occasion and develop
sound voting practices to promote?
In this season we find 5.4 million cases of COVID-19, and
170,000+ deaths in our nation.
We will ultimately get past this pandemic, yet this is not the
time to leave our voting rights as objects of deliberation.

BASIC NEEDS

August 28, 2020

During 2020 many find themselves reverting to basic needs in life,
Hunkered down and/or experiencing some form of strife.
Think back to Psychology 101
During carefree school days when, as far as worries go, we may
      have had little or none.

If we rack our brains, we might remember Maslow's hierarchy of
      needs.
A motivational theory indicating higher level needs can't be
      satisfied until we fulfill each level that precedes.
Shaped like a pyramid those needs come into view in the recesses
      of our minds,
From the bottom: physiological, safety, love and belonging,
      esteem, and self-actualization--the needs we, consciously or
      unconsciously, seek through the life we unwind.

Level One physiological needs like food, water, warmth, and rest
Must be met before we seek Level Two safety needs akin to
      security and safety as we progress.
Belongingness and love at Level Three translate into intimate
      relationships and friends with whom we are blessed.
Next, we may seek Level Four esteem needs such as prestige or
      feelings of accomplishment as we try to do our best.

Finally, some may seek Level Five self-fulfillment needs
      compatible with self-actualization where we seek to achieve
      our fullest potential as we crest.
According to Maslow, though, we cannot crest at Level Five until
      Level Four needs are met, otherwise our systems will
      experience unrest.
Likewise, without reaching Levels One, Two, and Three, to Level
      Four we cannot progress.
Human beings must have basic needs met before higher needs can
      be addressed.

Before 2020 many may have been living in comfortable homes
    with their food, water, shelter needs more than met.
Feeling safe, secure and enjoying cherished family relationships
    and friendships seemingly forever set.
Perhaps the raising of families in secure environments, careers, or
    volunteer work provided good feelings of accomplishment,
Or, maybe some were on their way to achieving their full potential
    in life with no regret.

As 2020 progressed, though, many jobs were threatened or lost,
Worries arose about feeding families, potential evictions, and
    nightmares of streets where belongings are tossed.
U.S. COVID cases rose to 5.8 million and deaths to 180,000+ so
    higher level needs succumb to security as we hunker down.
Fears that our families, friends, or ourselves will catch COVID
    abound.

Is there no wonder, why there is so much worry and anxiety?
Pervading our heretofore perceived exemplary society?
Aren't we living through a world-wide pandemic without
    contemporary precedent?
Our economy has certainly contracted, yet whether a deep
    recession is ahead experts with predictions are hesitant.

There is much uncertainty today.
Each and every aspect of life is affected in some way.
Will our loved ones get COVID-19 as summer turns to fall?
Will we go to sleep one night and end up as a 911 COVID call?

Will children be going back to school or not?
Will they attend in-person, online, or a hybrid, and how will they
    be taught?
Will we be able to find day care in the midst of the chaos?
Will employers hold out or will we suffer job loss?

Will we be able to put food on our table?
Will our lives ever be stable?
Will we be evicted if we can't pay our rent?
Will we have to go to a shelter or pitch a tent?

Will we be able to afford health care if we lose our jobs?
Will we wait in line for COVID-19 tests among the mobs?
Will our children suffer from anxiety and stress?
Will college graduates be able to pay off their student loans
    without jobs and redress?

Will crime increase as needs escalate?
Will foreclosures mount as the ability to pay mortgages
    evaporates?
Will small businesses that have closed ever come back?
Will shopping malls become re-purposed as online merchants rise
    and local stores crack?

Where ever many of us were in life prior to COVID-19,
We may revert back to Maslow's Level 1 physiological needs,
    previously unforeseen.
Those of us who are able, can consider opening up our hearts,
To help those who need food, water, shelter and try to do our part.

JOHN MCCAIN

August 29, 2020

On August 29 we commemorate the anniversary of the birth of
    John McCain,
A man who became a war hero and a U.S. Senator so many
    acclaim,
Born on this day in 1936 at Coco Solo Naval Station in the Panama
    Canal Zone
Where the McCain family was stationed, then under American
    control, their temporary home.

Senator McCain came from a military family,
Both his father and his paternal grandfather serving as four-star
    admirals dutifully.
In their footsteps he followed, graduating from the U.S. Naval
    Academy in 1958.
McCain graduated from flight school two years later, soon after
    which volunteer service in Vietnam became his fate.

On October 26, 1967 over the North Vietnamese capital of Hanoi
McCain's plane was shot down during a bombing run where he
    was deployed.
When a crash ensued, he broke both arms and one leg,
Later he was moved to a prison nicknamed the "Hanoi Hilton," a
    fate frighteningly vague.

When his captors learned of his family's military background, they
    offered him early release.
For a number of personal and military reasons he refused, whereby
    his subsequent pain did not cease.
McCain spent five and a half years in prisons, three and a half in
    solitary confinement.
He was tortured and beaten with no realignment.

On March 14, 1973 he was finally released along with other
American POWs from the war.
He earned the Silver Star, Bronze Star, Purple Heart, Distinguished
Flying Cross, in addition to respect, honor and more.
After working in his father-in-law's business, he served in the
House of Representatives for two terms where his name
became part of the Arizona political mix.
When longtime Arizona Senator Barry Goldwater retired, McCain
won this open U.S. Senate seat in 1986.

McCain built a strong leadership role in politics but also a
reputation for being somewhat of a maverick.
He debated his points with vigor always determined to make them
stick.
McCain stood up for what he believed and advocated for his
espoused strong positions,
Even if it meant promoting policies of his own party's opposition.

McCain ran for President but was defeated by Barack Obama in
2008.
Afterwards, despite suffering life-threatening illnesses he
continued to have a say in the debate.
On August 25, 2018, just a few days before his birthday, of
glioblastoma John Sidney McCain III died.
We can pray that one day again such an honorable man will abide.

LABOR DAY

September 7, 2020

Today is Labor Day, a holiday traditionally observed on the first
Monday in September,
Honoring American workers, their accomplishments,
contributions, successes we remember.
Conceived by the labor movement, Labor Day became a federal
holiday in 1894,
Celebrated in cities and towns across America from shore to shore.

Typically, Labor Day celebrations include picnics, parties, parades,
fireworks, and more.
It remains to be seen whether celebrations will be tampered down in
2020 due to the ongoing COVID-19 war.
For Americans Labor Day marks the end of the summer and
beginning of back-to-school seasons.
But the true conception of Labor Day resulted for profound reasons.

In the United States at the height of the Industrial Revolution,
Average Americans worked 12-hour days, seven days a week to eke
out a living and family financial contributions.
In some states, children worked in mills, factories, and mines at the
ages of five or six.
They toiled like adults earning only a fraction of adult wages in the
mix.

The poorest of the poor and immigrants suffered to no end.
With exposure to polluted air, unsanitary conditions, and no work
breaks they had to contend.
As the country progressed from an agrarian to a manufacturing
nation,
First appearing in the 18th century, labor unions grew in prominence
since their formation.

This was a time in American history when unions organized strikes
and rallies to protest poor working conditions,
Pushing employers to negotiate better wages and hours without
inhibition.
However, events like the Haymarket Riot became violent in 1886.
Both workers and policemen were killed, despite efforts to nix.

On May 11, 1894 employees of Chicago's Pullman Palace Car
Company went on strike
To protest wage cuts, firing of union workers, and the like.
Nearly six weeks later on June 26 the American Railroad Union led
by Eugene V. Debs
Boycotted Pullman railway cars, creating a crippling railroad traffic
web.

As the government moved to break the Pullman strike,
Forces were dispatched to Chicago including thousands of federal
and state troops, police officers, and deputy marshals alike.
Ensuing violence resulted in more wounded and dead.
Eventually the strike ended, troops left, trains resumed, and the
violence abated.

In the midst of these massive protests, parades, and unrest, Labor
Day was born.
On June 28, 1894 President Grover Cleveland signed the holiday
into law, perhaps to calm the forlorn.
The true founder of Labor Day is still an open and debated question.
Peter J. McGuire, cofounder of the American Federation of Labor,
and Matthew Maguire, a secretary of the Central Labor Union,
are two historical suggestions.

What will the Labor Day celebrations of 2020 mark?

Due to COVID-19 and job loss, do workers fear their futures are in the dark?

Noting 6.3 million COVID-19 cases and 189,000+ related deaths, will furloughed individuals join the ranks of the unemployed, necessitating job search requests?

Will we combat COVID-19 spread and restore our economy so all who want to work can do so, earning wages that are not repressed?

PEACE DAY

September 21, 2020

Observed on September 21 is the International Day of Peace.
It was established in 1981 by the United Nations General
      Assembly as a way to enable worldwide conflicts to cease.
Symbolized by a white peace dove with an olive branch in its beak,
The emblem also viewed as a *personal* peace offering--one
      person to another may seek.

In past years various events were organized to commemorate
      Peace Day.
Concerts, picnics, interfaith ceremonies, prayers, candle lightings
      occurred in a public or a private way.
Each year since its inception Peace Day promotes the observation
      of 24 hours of non-violence and cease fire.
On Peace Day 2020 to what should we aspire?

COVID-19 threatens our health, our safety, and our way of life.
What manifests in one part of the country or the world can cause
      far reaching strife.
Don't all people now share a common enemy in COVID-19?
Can fighting against the virus unite us even if the battle was once
      unforeseen?

On September 21, 2020 we mark 31,100,000+ COVID-19 cases
      worldwide.
And due to our common enemy, 962,000+ victims in the world
      have died.
Our U.S. case count rose to 6,826,000+ from COVID-19.
Nearly 200,000 have died including old, young, and in-between.

Months into this battle we still dwell on concepts arising long ago,
Masks—Recommended? Mandated? Discarded? Friend or foe?
Promotion of herd immunity through disease spread with no other
    strategy to share?
Wouldn't this result in millions more deaths and potential
    apocalyptic despair?

Let's hope the last quarter of 2020
Will alleviate stress from the masses who have experienced plenty.
Together, thinking clearly on behalf of all citizens, can we unite
    and try to weather this storm?
Through the 2020 theme of "Shaping Peace Together," can we
    enable compassion and hope to become the norm?

RBG

September 23, 2020

In the midst of our ever-changing status quo, we mourn the death
  of Ruth Bader Ginsburg, who died on September 18 in her
  home at the age of 87.
RBG, as she was known, became a legal, cultural, and feminist
  icon who used her intellect as a weapon,
Since the early 1970s, she arose as an architect of a legal fight
In the promotion of equality and women's rights.

Despite graduating at the top of her class at Ivy League schools,
  law firm jobs were closed to women, like other opportunities.
But RBG wasn't willing to accept this disunity in legal
  communities.
In 1963 she was hired to teach at Rutgers Law School, and not
  long after she began fighting gender discrimination.
Behind her soft voice and large glasses, she demonstrated
  considerable determination.

RBG founded the Women's Rights Project at the American Civil
  Liberties Union.
The battle for women's rights became a type of legal communion.
She became the first tenured professor at Columbia Law School,
  another part of her evolution.
A cautious legal scholar, she focused singularly on her goal of
  winning, which sparked her legal revolution.

Serving 27 years on the Supreme Court of our land,
RBG became a rock star featured in film, operetta, merchandise,
  SNL sketches—all in the RBG brand.
RBG's passing we continue to mourn,
In the midst of a new battle recently born.

In 2016, for nearly a year, the opposition party refused to consider
    President Barack Obama's Supreme court nominee under the
    auspices of it being an election year.
Now, in 2020 the tables have turned with the election a mere six
    weeks away and stirring fear.
Will the opposition party refuse to follow the course they set as
    some of their members have made clear?
In the midst of a flaring COVID-19, we have chaos ringing
    through each ear.

Despite the election year cacophony and sanctimonious operettas
    on high,
Let's not forget this admirable, praiseworthy woman who deserves
    a heartfelt goodbye.
The eloquence of her words, the fecundity of her legal scholarship,
    the passion of her mission
Should not be overshadowed by ricocheting decrees, edicts,
    pledges, and vows sowing division.

IS THE WORLD FLAT?

October 12, 2020

On the second Monday in October we observe Columbus Day,
Commemorating the voyage and landing of Christopher Columbus
    in the New World, now a federal holiday in the USA.
Like all men, Columbus had strengths and weaknesses, whereby
    his accomplishments have been subject to debate,
But his discovery of the New World is generally not a subject to
    repudiate.

On Columbus Day 2020, what if individuals proposed, proffered,
    or purported the world is flat?
Would we consider the concept placed in motion by a jokester, a
    prankster, or a wisecracking tautological acrobat?
What if this message was declared in a strident manner and a
    truculent voice?
Or, if the concept was commercialized by a mega millionaire in a
    chauffeur-driven Rolls Royce?

When traveling the world would we then expect the land mass or
    the ocean to simply end?
Or, would we challenge the flat world contention through analysis
    and evaluation so we could better comprehend?
Would we buy into the idea of a flat world and try to convince a
    relative or a friend?
Or, would we slyly laugh to ourselves while promoting a flat world
    as a truth we'd pretend?

Didn't the scholars of old and the ancient Greeks believe a flat
    world was a fallacy?
Didn't Christopher Columbus persuade King Ferdinand and Queen
    Isabella of Spain to sponsor his explorations west with
    alacrity?

Didn't Columbus land on a small island in the Bahamas on
    October 12, 1492, convinced he had reached Asia—his
    ultimate destination?
Didn't Columbus, and other explorers who discovered the
    Americas, accept the theory that the world was round—a
    concept once beyond imagination?

On this Columbus Day do we view the year 2020 as devastatingly
    strange?
Who could have predicted a pandemic, an economic crisis,
    social unrest, and, perhaps, a constitutional crisis that may
    make us feel estranged?
Ten months into the pandemic, are we still debating the validity of
    masking?
Why are some individuals disbanding masks and social distancing,
    others continue asking?

Will we have an efficacious vaccine this year?
If a vaccine is without sufficient efficacy, would this erode trust
    and foster fear?
Hasn't our U.S. case count risen to 7.7 million due to COVID-19?
Haven't nearly 215,000 souls died--old, young, and in-between?

Yet, why do we continue to hear the pandemic is just a hoax?
Is life "business as usual" for some folks?
Why do people in positions of power urge us to believe COVID-19
    is part of the past?
Is herd immunity, before implementation of a vaccine, a pipe
    dream or a solution at long last?

How do we assimilate current debates about science and our
    country's resulting division?
Why do some feel disarmed and worry about our democracy being
    threatened by a constitutional collision?
How do we absorb the vehemence of positions decried by those
    willing to combat?
Or, do we ponder whether half of our nation believes the world is
    flat?

HALLOWEEN

October 31, 2020

On October 31 each year we celebrate Halloween.
This children's holiday has a history both prescient and
    unforeseen.
The tradition dates back to the ancient Celts who, while wearing
    costumes, lit bonfires
To ward off ghosts that fright inspires.

In the eighth century under Pope Gregory III, on November 1,
    All Saints Day was born.
On All Hallows Eve, the evening before, the saints were mourned.
Years passed and before long Halloween evolved into a fun day of
    trick-or-treating.
Wearing costumes, carving jack-o-lanterns, children gathered
    candy in Halloween bags for hoarding and eating.

This Halloween the world is in a confused and frightened state.
COVID-19 case counts rising to 9.1 million in the US and
    45.9 million in the world don't seem to abate.
Uncertainty is in the air.
Due to unemployment projections people feel despair.

Questions loom as individuals worry about a recession.
Contrarians question whether a recession could lead the
    interdependent global financial system into a depression.
Is there an economy in the world that has not declined?
How will the slowdown in growth affect trade, imports, exports,
    tariffs--all so intertwined?

What is the future of work as we know it?
Will workers return to offices? Or continue working from home
    until employers see fit?
Will all workers who were "temporarily" furloughed have jobs to
    return to?
How many small businesses will close for good, awaiting
    government bailouts now overdue?

Will people be willing to travel on planes and trains as frequently
    as in the past?
Will the hospitality industry endure for long last?
Will activities involving crowds be out of bounds for the
    foreseeable future?
Will the world's competitive marketplace need surgery and
    sutures?

Are countries in danger of defaulting on debt?
How will developing countries' vulnerabilities be met?
How will health systems fare during the next wave of COVID-19?
For wealthy countries, poor countries, and those in-between?

Is a sustainable long-term economic recovery possible until the
    virus is fully contained?
Does containment mean a vaccine must be fully developed with
    a designated efficacy maintained?
Who will receive the vaccine first and who will follow?
Will some decline an effective vaccine, promoting myths that ring
    hollow?

More questions than answers face us this Halloween.
Scary stories create a frightening scene.
Like militias allegedly conspiring to kidnap a governor and cause
    her deleterious harm.
Threats of blowing up buildings, groups armed at polling places,
    neighbor striking neighbor when asked to wear a mask--all
    cause for alarm.

On Halloween we conjure up skeletons, witches, and big black
    bats,
But aren't 1.1 million deaths in the world and 230,000+ in the
    USA far more frightening than a few black cats?
Deaths surpass those of WWI, WWII, the Civil War, and many
    others.
While unrest in our country pits brothers against brothers.

Spine-chilling, spooky stories sound eerie and creepy.
Imagine blood-curdling yells and potions making us sleepy.
But the scariest story this Halloween day,
May be the fright we are living here in the USA.

THANKSGIVING DAY

November 26, 2010

Thanksgiving Day is a national holiday, originating in 1621 as an
    autumn harvest feast,
Among the Plymouth colonists and the Wampanoag Indians
    goodwill was released.
Today many will enjoy turkey, stuffing, cranberry sauce, and
    pumpkin pie,
Perhaps, with fewer guests and avoidance of last Thanksgiving
    Day's conversations that drew the roll of an eye.

Through centuries Thanksgiving Day continued to be celebrated,
A sharing of meals with family and friends--among Americans a
    holiday highly rated.
In 1863 during the middle of the Civil War, Abraham Lincoln
    made this day one to remember.
He proclaimed a national Thanksgiving Day to be held each
    November.

The year 2020 has been an unusual year to say the least.
We have been fighting this virus, often resembling an
    incomprehensible beast.
12,879,000+ individuals have been victim to COVID-19 in
    the USA.
263,000+ mothers', fathers', sisters', brothers' seats will be empty
    this Thanksgiving Day.

Despite the challenges of this year there is much for which we give
    thanks.
Several vaccines are on the horizon with potential distribution in
    the flanks.
The conundrum of manufacturing, sourcing of supplies, and
    storage at excessively low temperatures still hover about.
Delivery to billions of people throughout the world still needs to be
    worked out.

The months seem eternal as we anxiously await an efficacious
    vaccine.
Let us not forget the inception of the polio epidemic occurring in
    1916.
39 years of trial and error passed before Dr. Jonas Salk achieved
    success—once unforeseen.
Can we fathom what decades of dealing with looming COVID-19
    threats would mean?

Through faith, hope, and reliance on science citizens will work this
    out.
Can we remain strong in our convictions and resist disinformation
    promoting doubt?
Can we recognize a pandemic for what it is, along with its
    perceived threats and stress?
Can we refrain from succumbing to follies in the quagmire of our
    ubiquitous game of chess?

Focus on COVID-19 has become an international obsession,
    rightfully so,
But we cannot forget the everyday blessings we sow.
In troubling times, despair can overwhelm and be difficult to
    forego,
Yet blessings emerge from on high to bestow.

For what we give thanks is a personal vow,
Expressed to each other or through our inner sanctum to thee or
    thou.
Let us pray the goodness we possess
Will help us give thanks as we emerge from the year of 2020's
    darkness.

GOOD-BYE 2020

December, 2020

During the last month of each year, we revere the holidays many
    celebrate.
Contemporaneously, this December 2020 provides opportunities to
    step back and ruminate,
About aspects of a year, we may want to repudiate or obliterate,
But not venerate or commemorate.

On January 1, 2020 we rang in the new year,
Wishing our friends and family good cheer.
Weeks passed before we started to hear
About a mysterious virus that humans should fear.

U.S. travel to China halted and we asked experts to expound.
Stories of a deadly virus passing from animals to humans in a
    Wuhan market began to abound.
While those sick were in need of dire care, medical staff had no
    PPE to spare.
Suddenly COVID-19-stricken patients were in ICUs needing
    critical care.

In our new lexicon, terms like "social distancing" emerged as
    COVID-19 cases reached new peaks.
On May 27, 100,000 COVID-19 deaths occurred in the USA in
    just 12 weeks.
Five months later death counts doubled despite salubrious
    treatment tweaks.
We prayed for a vaccine while scientists labored in developing
    therapeutic techniques.

As the pandemic enveloped us, we faced reports of unarmed black
    men's deaths, social unrest, economic stress, and questions
    causing fear.
Why were Confederate flags and bounties on the heads of our
    military such hot topics this year?
What happened to the children separated from families
    at the border not long ago?
Have they been returned to family members? Does anyone know?

Why did testing myths dominate discussions throughout the year?
Why couldn't we get beyond the swabs, reagents, lab licensing in
    order to alleviate fear?
Why were some COVID-19 tests processed in an hour or less?
While others required more than two weeks at best?

In 2020 why was wearing of masks under continual scrutiny?
We acknowledge that most men and women want to be free.
Who chooses lock-up, lock-out, lock-down by mandate or decree?
Isn't it incumbent upon all of us to balance individual rights, public
    safety, and humanity?

In 2020 some promoted voter fraud as a national scare,
Even when a number of studies confirmed that any type of voting
    fraud is rare.
For weeks, it seemed like the totality of what we heard
Was COVID and voting—no other word.

Why did voting by mail become front and center for this year's
    election sessions?
Absentee ballots have been used for years without transgressions.
Why was mail-in voting portrayed as "illegal," creating a
    confusing impression?
How many times did we have to discuss voter suppression?

Why, during a pandemic, was our postal service under attack?
Why were various mail sorting machines removed from post
     offices despite the flack?
Why did narratives of postal slowdowns sound off like drumbeats
     across our nation?
During an election year and a pandemic--why such a fixation?

On July 17, 2020 the world lost an iconic humble man.
Who could match his kindness, empathy, and willingness to lend a
     hand?
We are grateful to know bequeathed to us who remain
Is a mentor, John Lewis, who provides a path to follow on our
     challenging terrain.

Then, nearly two months later on September 18, RBG left us
     amidst the election year cacophonic operettas on high.
Can we ever forget this admirable, praiseworthy woman who
     deserved a heartfelt goodbye?
The eloquence of her words, the fecundity of her legal scholarship
     and the passion of her mission
Seemed to be overshadowed by ricocheting decrees, edicts,
     pledges and vows sowing division.

As December ends 83,140,000+ COVID-19 victims in the world
     and 19,850,000+ in the USA, leave many in despair.
Worried about COVID-19, jobs, health insurance, food, rent, or
     whether anyone will care.
Although Europe fought the first COVID-19 wave with force,
It struggles in the clutches of the second wave with little recourse.

December brings good news of two vaccines in the USA.
The first country to move forward was the UK.
Yet, in the USA worries persist about public trust in the vaccine,
And whether the path to herd immunity can become routine.

Deaths climb to 1,810,000+ in the world and 344,000+ in the USA.
Experts predict hundreds of thousands more may be on their way,
Before the world has weathered this storm,
And in the hope public health administrators get ready for reform.

During crises like wars and natural disasters alike,
Peoples of the world have found ways to unite.
Risking perilous perdition, will we allow chaotic divisiveness and
    demagoguery to assail?
Will denizens of democracy emerge from this thorny thicket,
    enabling our Constitution to prevail?

Americans rise above their challenges and seek to find their way.
With 2020 soon behind us, can we eradicate division and
    uphold our democracy as a country united one day?
Will our heroes and heroines teach us to promote justice in what
    we do, as well as what we say?
Can we walk humbly toward one another instead of going astray?

Good-bye 2020—that infamous year we may always remember but
    try to forget,
Good-bye 2020—close the door with a bang and imagine we never
    met.
Good-bye 2020—take COVID-19 with you along with social
    unrest, chaos, and disarray,
Good-bye 2020—let us look forward with hope toward 2021, bow
    our heads, and pray.

ABOUT THE AUTHOR

W. G. Perry is a poet, educator, history buff, and world traveler.

AUTHOR NOTE

A World Turned Upside Down chronicles noteworthy developments during 2020, a unique and unprecedented year, in which the world experienced the greatest health crisis of this century.

The first poem in *A World Turned Upside Down* was created as public awareness emerged about the novel coronavirus, now more commonly known as COVID-19. While ensuing weeks and months of 2020 flowed forward, significant events were memorialized in poems. Each poem notes the date of its creation. Any COVID-related data in the poems was derived from John Hopkins Center for Systems Science and Engineering on the day the poem was created.

The poems attempt to showcase historical markers, events, and societal issues recorded during 2020 as the nation faced this virulent pandemic amidst an era of social unrest, economic uncertainty, and challenges to our democracy.

While COVID-19 case counts grew, the effects on social events and traditional norms were undergoing upheaval during the commemoration of traditional holidays. This pattern was echoed in the poems as the year progressed.

Challenges experienced by health care personnel and essential workers enkindled a number of poems. Contemporaneously, the dilemmas involved in social unrest imbued others.

By year end, the collection of poems marked the melancholy experienced by some, while paying tribute to others, and extending hope to all.

As a reflection of the issues and challenges encountered during 2020, this collection of poetry presents thought-provoking questions for readers to absorb and on which they can ruminate.

W.G. Perry writes poetry for our times, the times in which we live.   If you would like to join an email list to learn about the release of additional poetry for our times created in 2021 and beyond, please email wgperrypoet@gmail.com.

~

If you enjoyed *A World Turned Upside Down*, consider leaving a short review on Amazon.com. Reviews are important sources of information and feedback. Thank you!

~

Thank you for your interest in *A World Turned Upside Down*.

ACKNOWLEDGEMENTS

I am grateful to Marcia who read "The Pandemic" after I sent it to her for a casual read. Her reaction encouraged me to write the next poem. I shared that one with her as well. One poem led to another. From that point forward she read each poem, suggested combining the poems to form a collection, and made insightful comments on the final draft.

~

I also wish to express my deep appreciation to an individual who knows who he is--a poetry aficionado who read and commented on each of the poems in this collection and encouraged the publishing of *A World Turned Upside Down.*

~

Likewise, I thank Sandy who read the collection and made helpful suggestions and comments.